ALFRED's SACRED PERFORMER SERIES

Hymns with a Velvet Touch

Arranged by Tom Fettke

10 Elegant Settings of Timeless Hymns

It is appropriate that my first keyboard project consists of 12 old friends—gospel hymns that have warmed my heart since childhood. I find these hymns to be both beautiful and profound. They were obviously written by individuals who were touched and inspired by Almighty God. I hope that these keyboard settings will warm your heart and bring pleasure to your ears and fingers.

Bless you,

	PAGE
ABIDE WITH ME	14
BE THOU MY VISION	30
DAY BY DAY	2
MORE LOVE TO THEE/I LOVE THEE	26
MY FAITH HAS FOUND A RESTING PLACE	18
MY FAITH LOOKS UP TO THEE	22
SAVIOR, LIKE A SHEPHERD LEAD US	38
SUN OF MY SOUL	34
TAKE MY LIFE AND LET IT BE/I SURRENDER ALL	10
TAKE TIME TO BE HOLY	6

Copyright © MMIV by Alfred Music Publishing Co., Inc.
All rights reserved. Printed in U.S.A.

Alfred

Day by Day

Words by Lina Sandell
Translated by Andrew L. Skoog

Day by day, and with each passing moment,
Strength I find, to meet my trials here;
Trusting in my Father's wise bestowment,
I've no cause for worry or for fear.
He Whose heart is kind beyond all measure
Gives unto each day what He deems best,
Lovingly, its part of pain and pleasure,
Mingling toil with peace and rest.

Oscar Ahnfelt
Arr. Tom Fettke

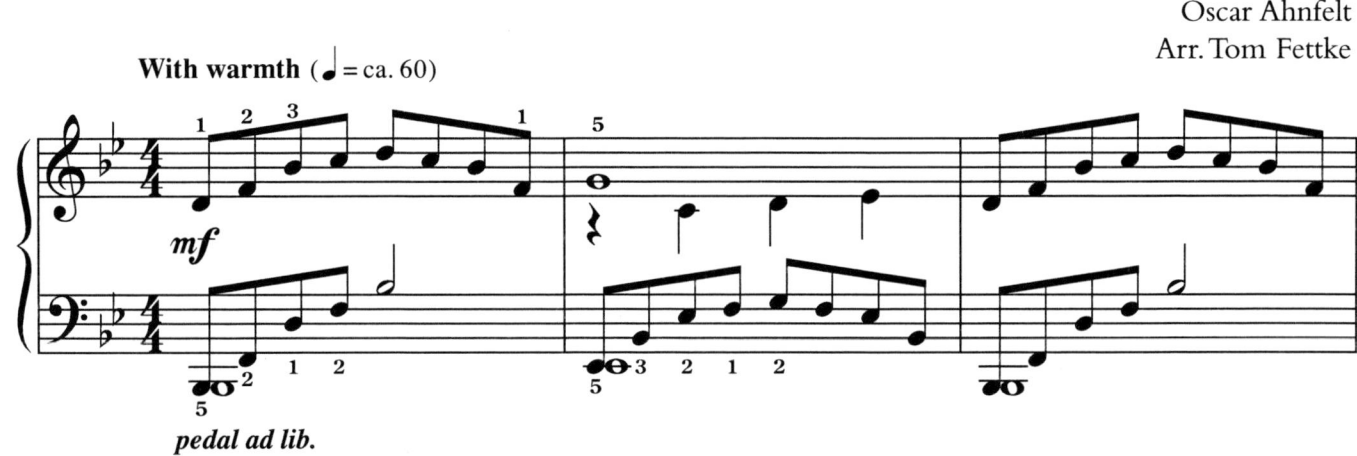

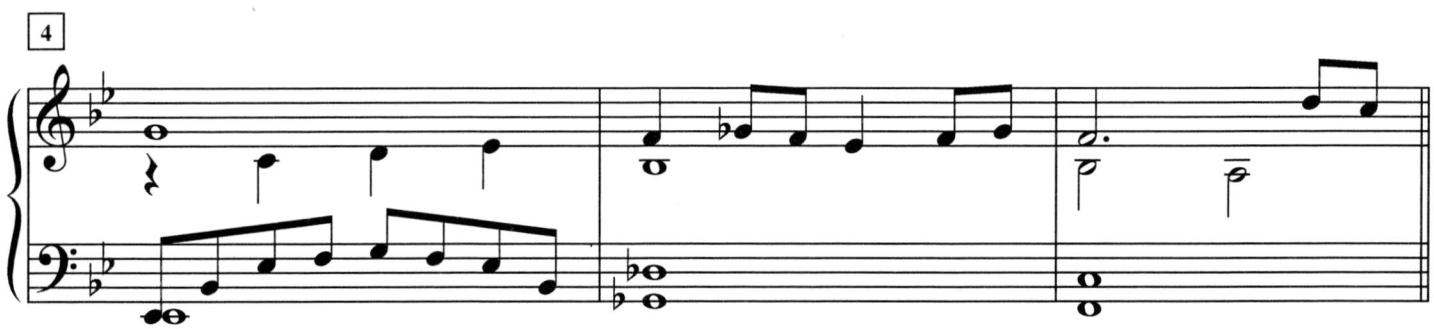

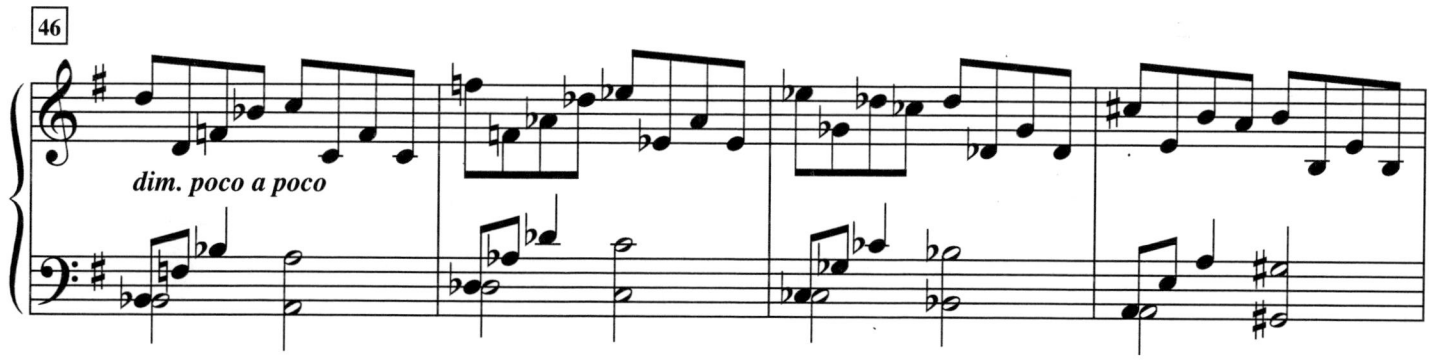
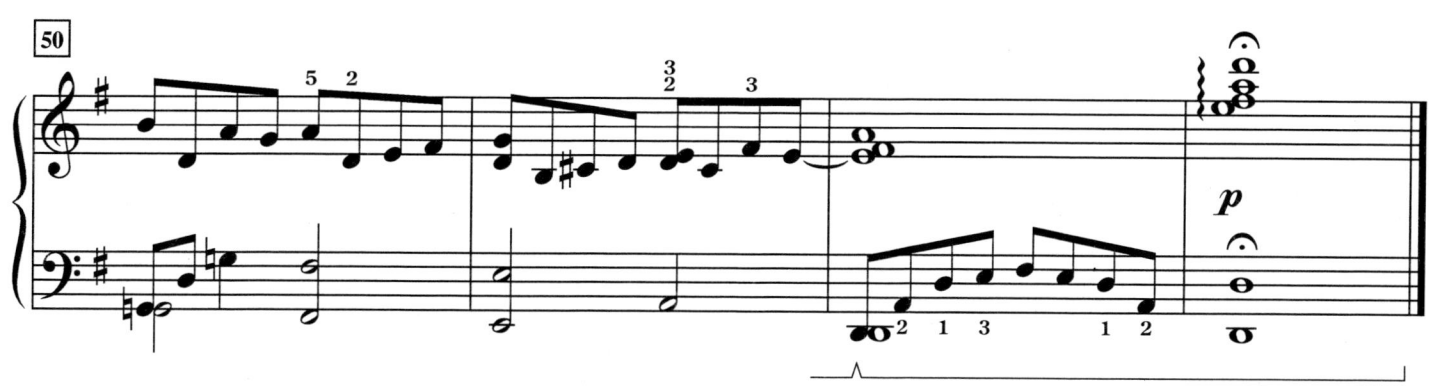

Take Time to Be Holy

Words by William D. Longstaff

Take time to be holy, speak oft with thy Lord;
Abide in Him always, and feed on His Word.
Make friends of God's children, help those who are weak,
Forgetting in nothing His blessing to seek.

George C. Stebbins
Arr. Tom Fettke

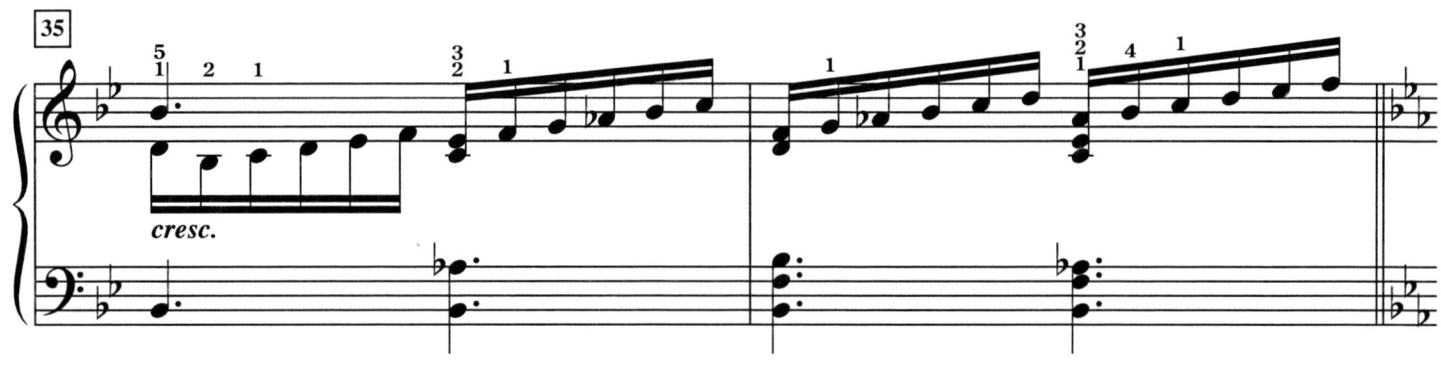

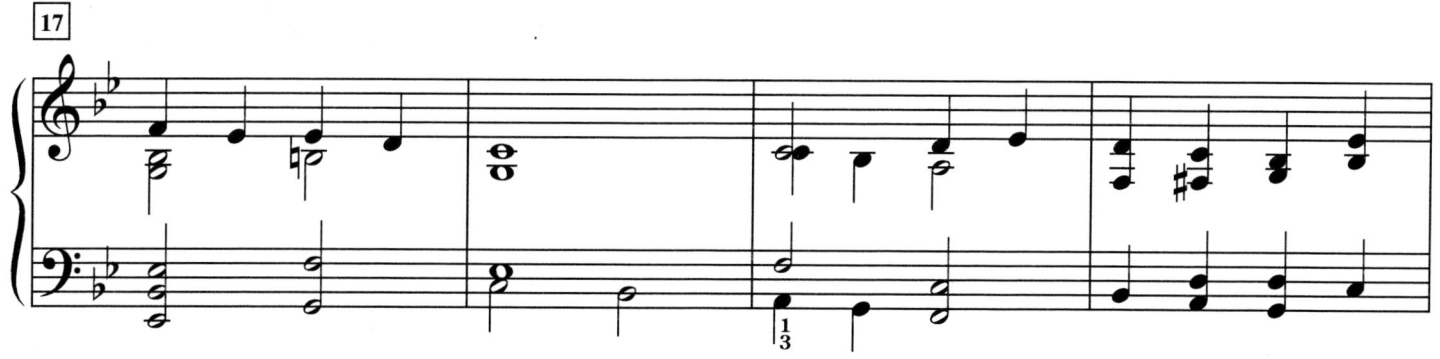
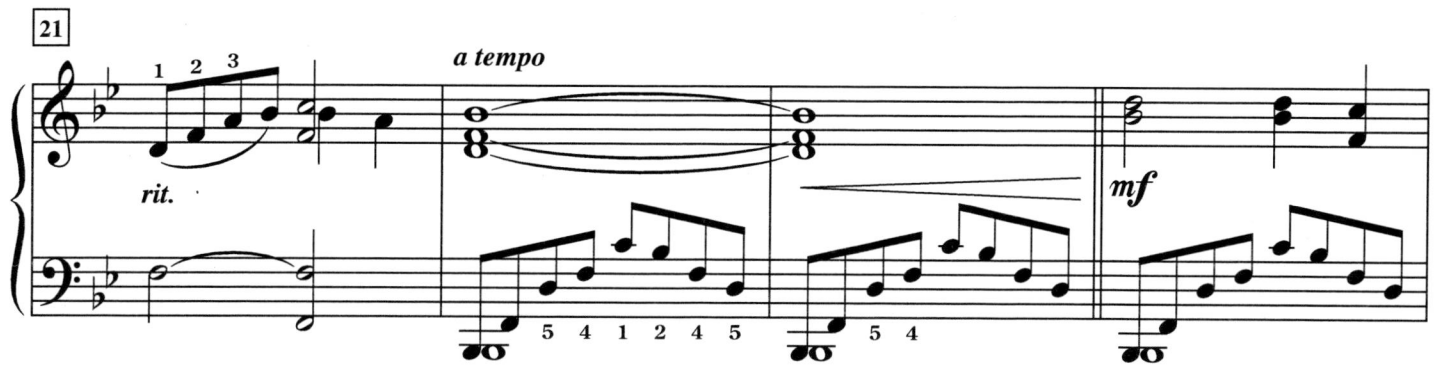
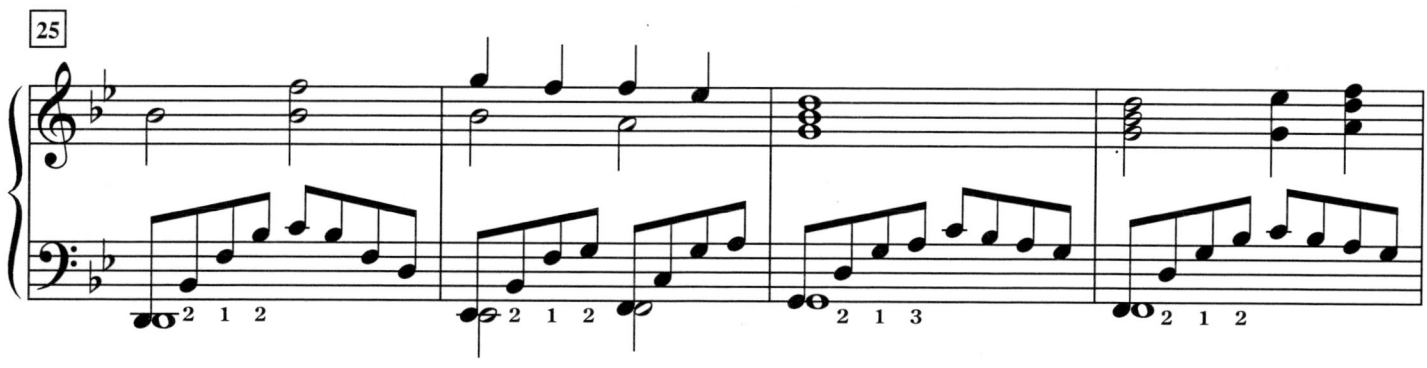

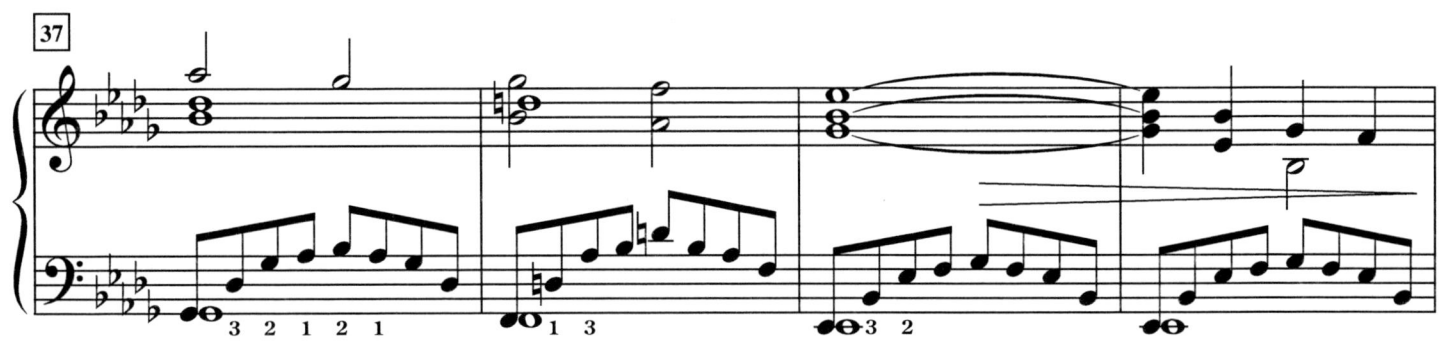

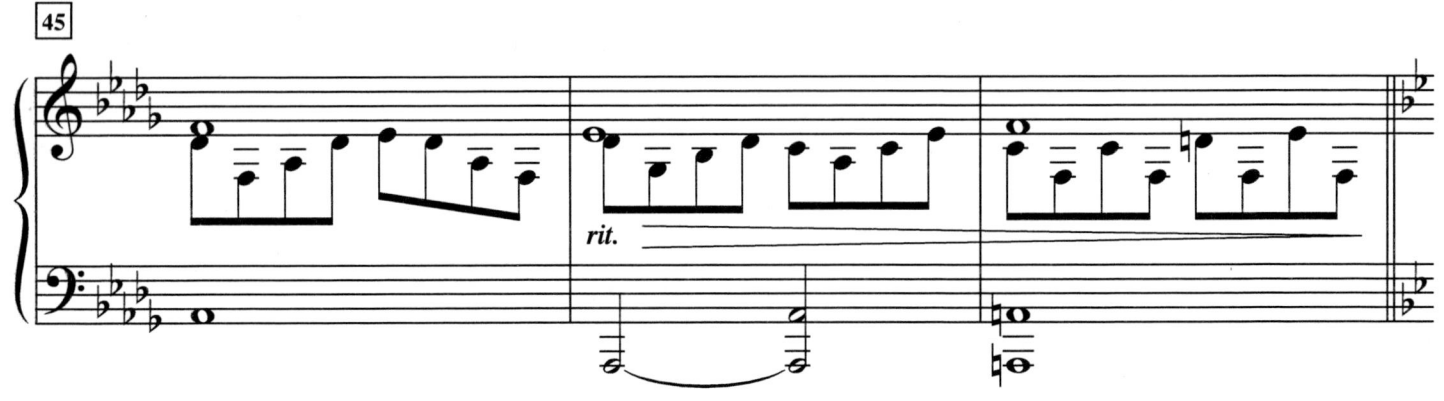

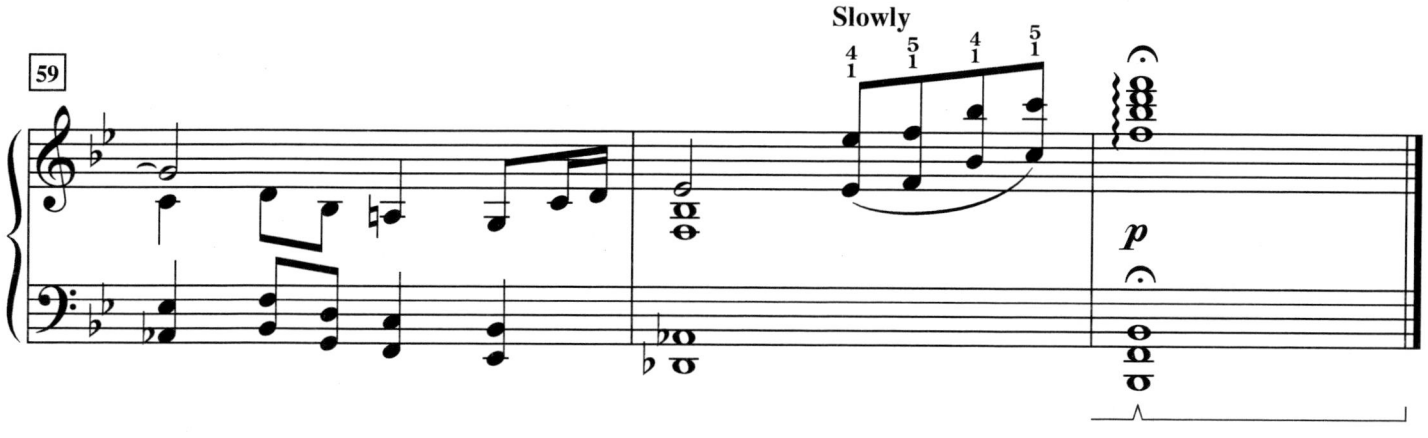

My Faith Has Found a Resting Place

Words by Eliza E. Hewitt

My faith has found a resting place, not in device or creed;
I trust the ever-living One; His wounds for me shall plead.

Refrain:
I need no other argument, I need no other plea;
It is enough that Jesus died, And that He died for me.

Norwegian folk melody
Arr. Tom Fettke

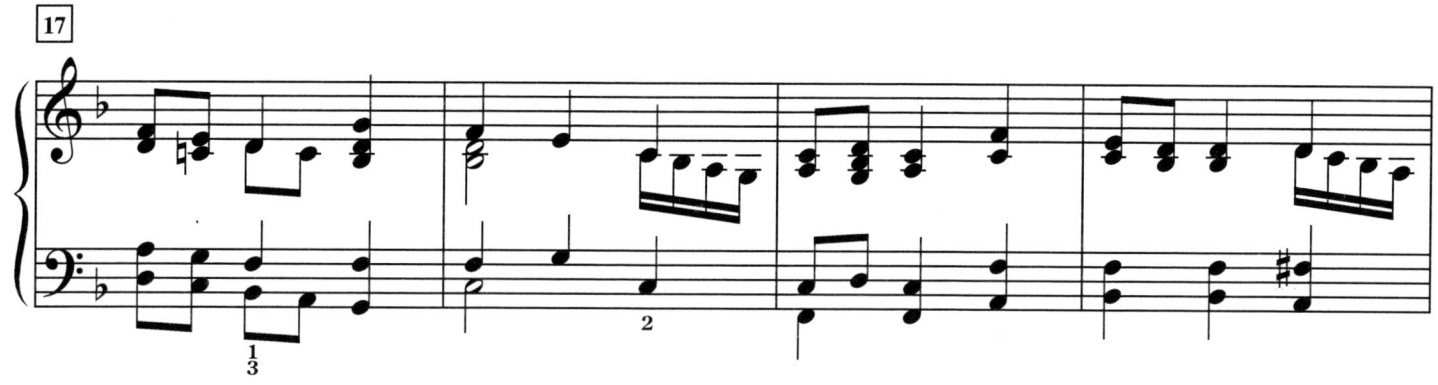

My Faith Looks Up to Thee

Words by Ray Palmer

My faith looks up to Thee,
Thou Lamb of Calvary, Savior divine!
Now hear me while I pray, take all my guilt away,
O let me from this day be wholly Thine!

Lowell Mason
Arr. Tom Fettke

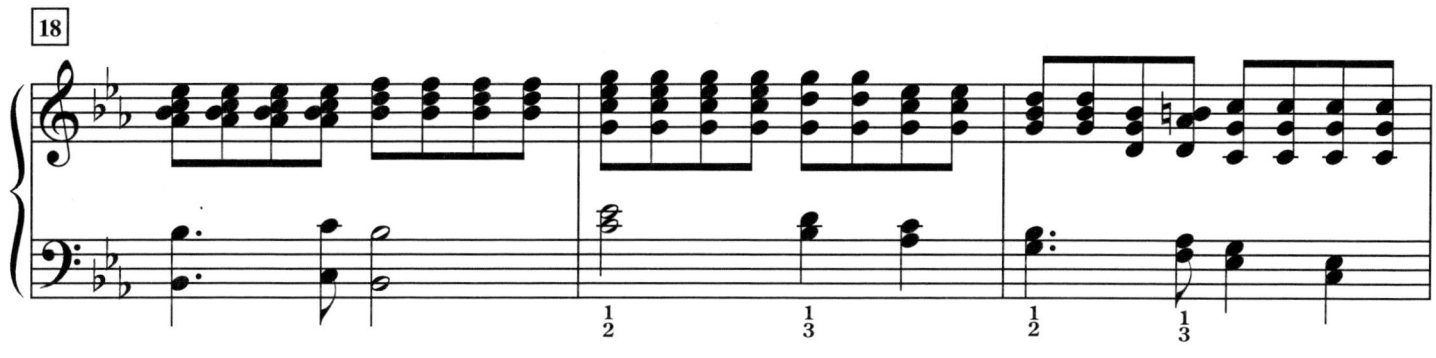
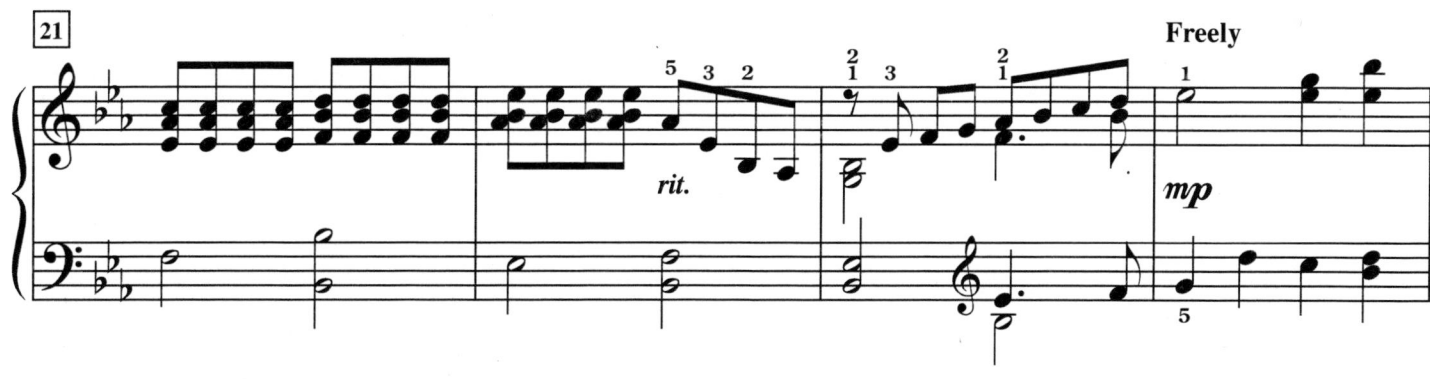
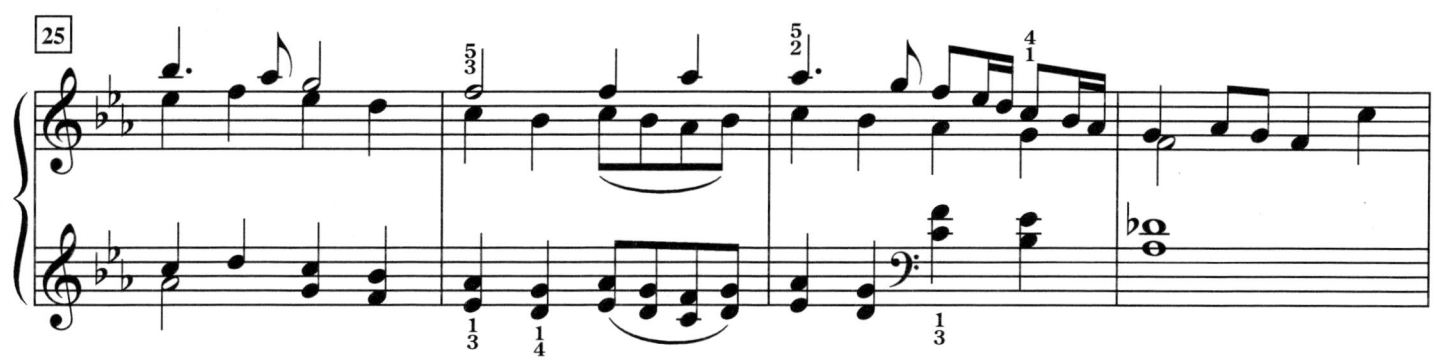

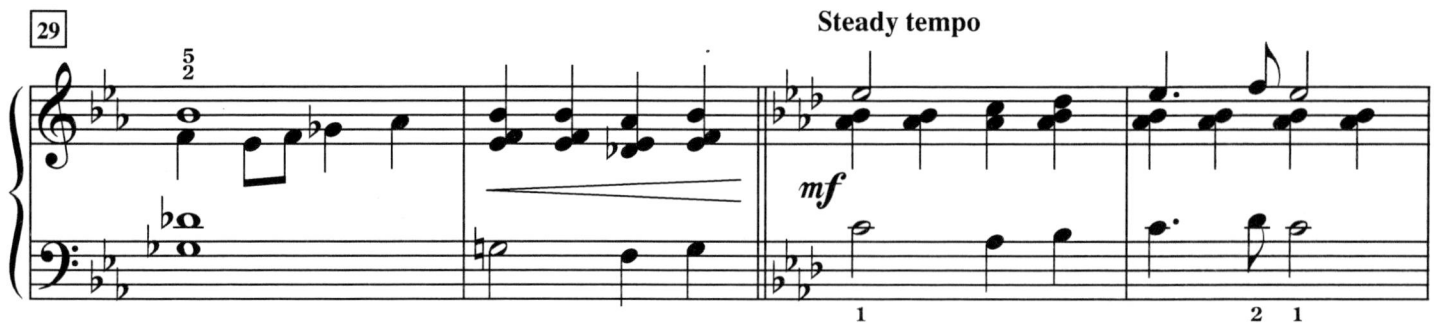

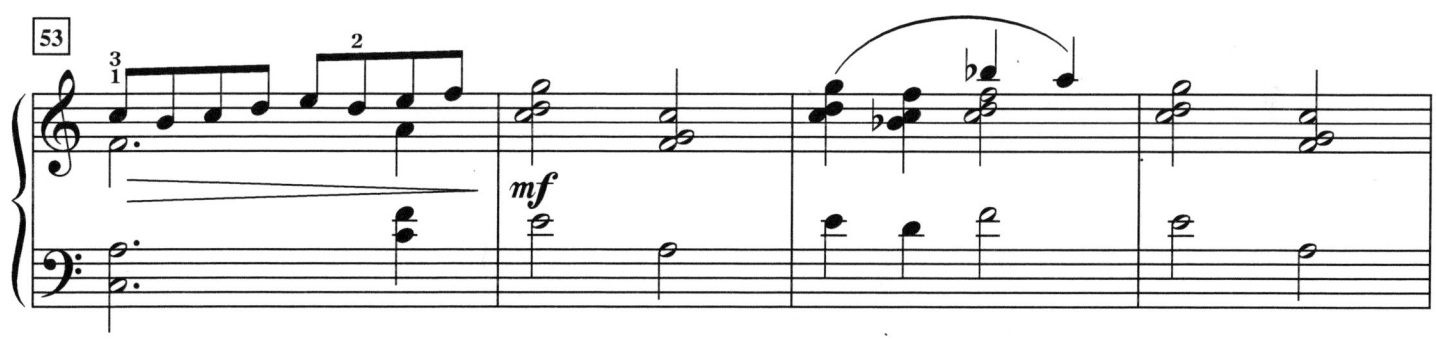

More Love to Thee
with "I Love Thee"

Words by Elizabeth P. Prentiss

More love to Thee, O Christ, more love to Thee!
Hear Thou the prayer I make on bended knee.
This is my earnest plea: More love, O Christ, to Thee,
More love to Thee, more love to Thee!

Words: Anonymous

I love Thee, I love Thee, I love Thee, my Lord;
I love Thee, my Savior, I love Thee, my God;
I love Thee, I love Thee, and that Thou dost know;
But how much I love Thee my actions will show.

William H. Doane
and from Ingall's *Christian Harmony*
Arr. Tom Fettke

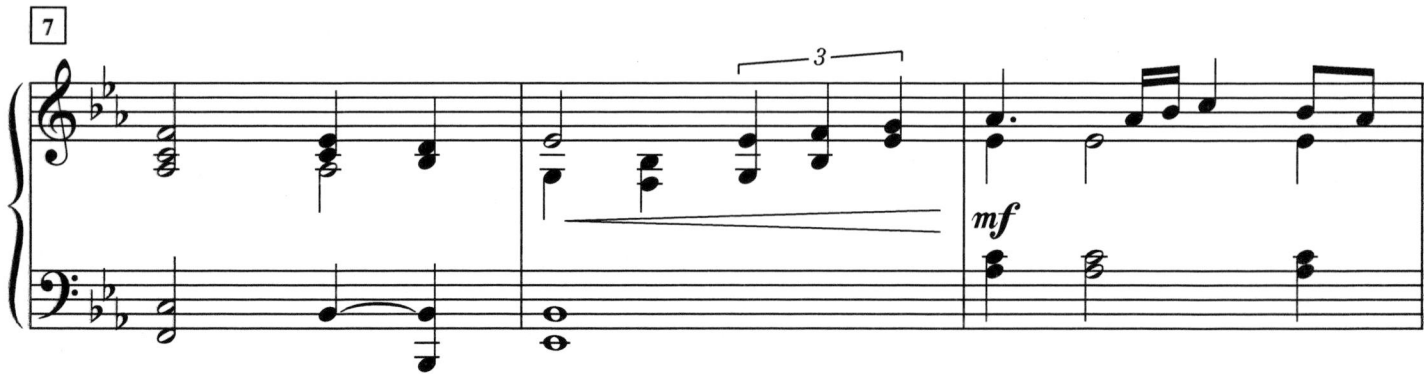

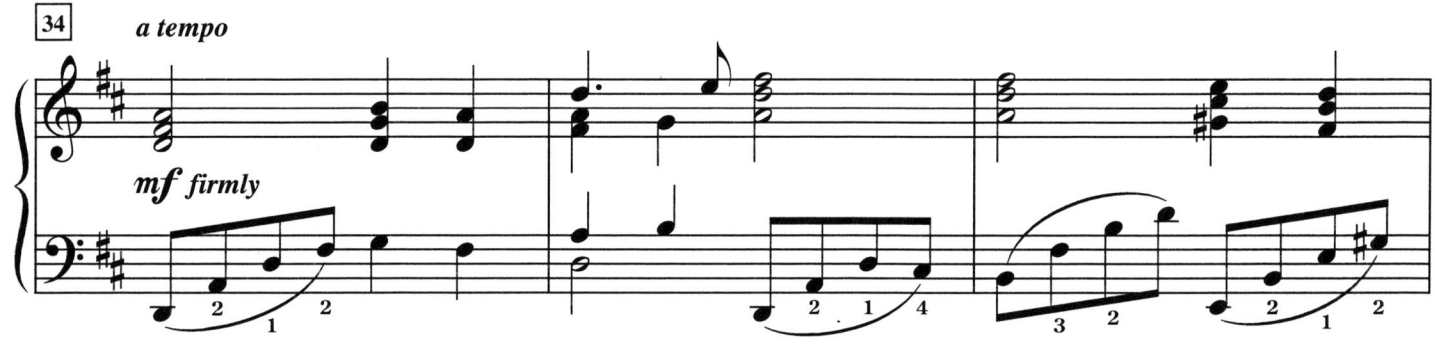
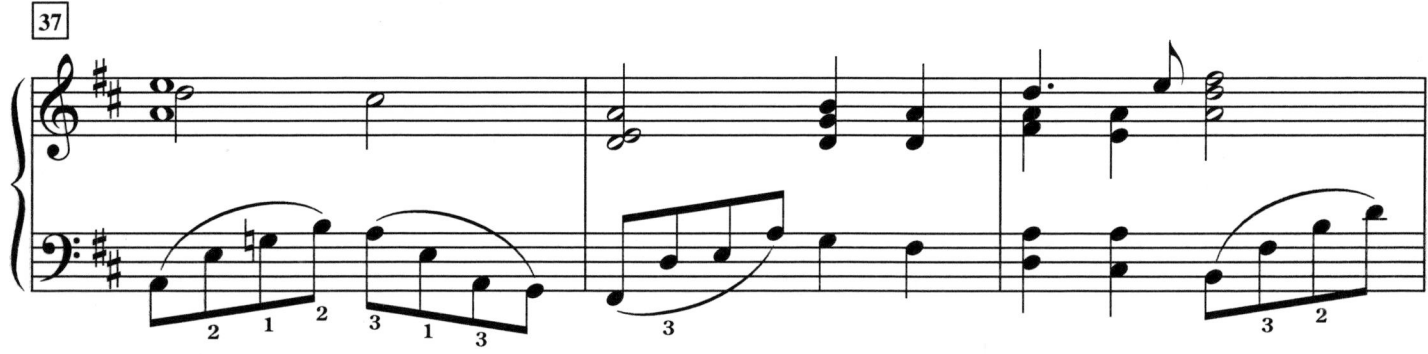
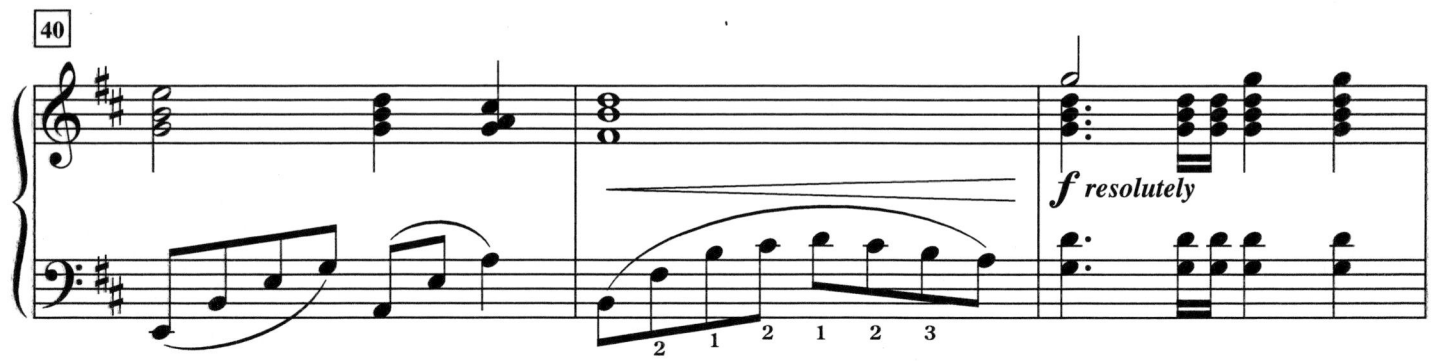

BE THOU MY VISION

Words: Attributed to Dallan Forgaill (8th Century)
Translated by Mary E. Byrne

Be Thou my Vision, O Lord of my heart;
Naught be all else to me, save that Thou art—
Thou my best thought, by day or by night,
Waking or sleeping, Thy presence my light.

Traditional Irish melody
Arr. Tom Fettke

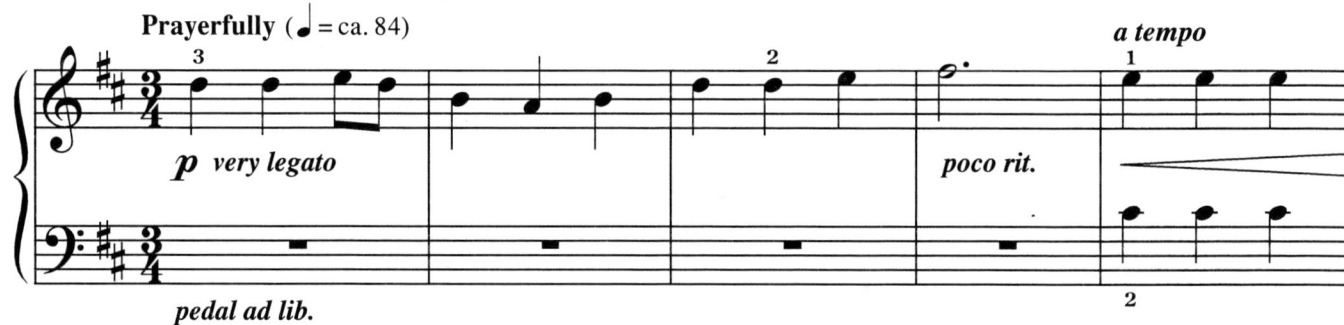

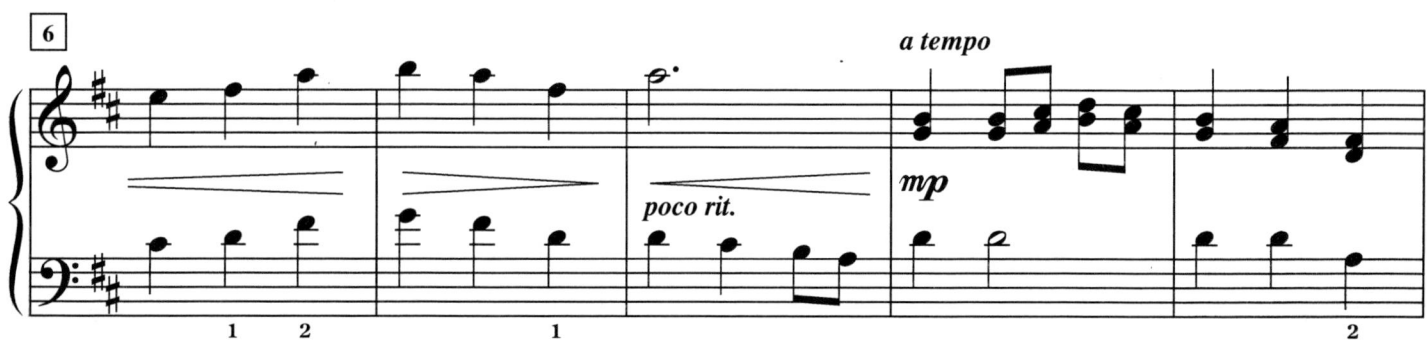

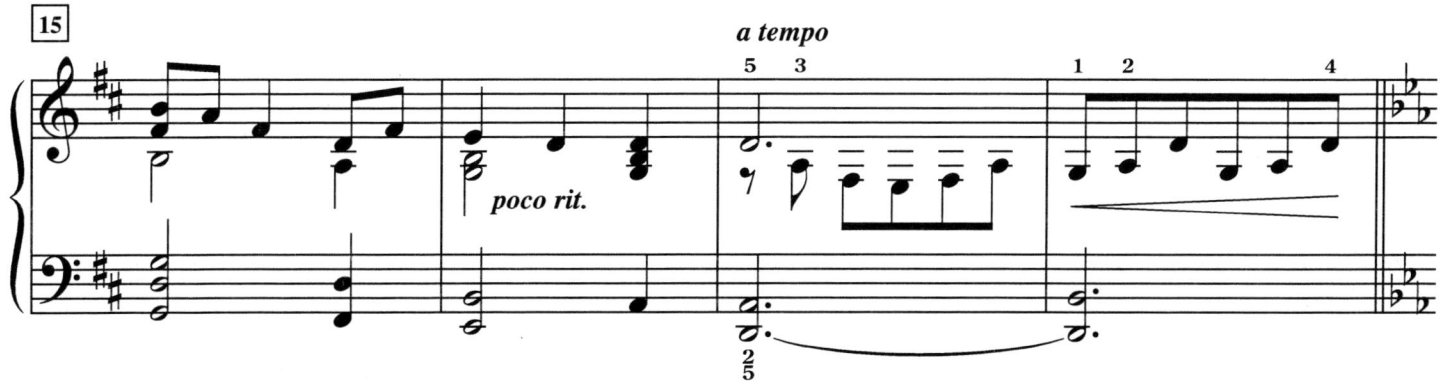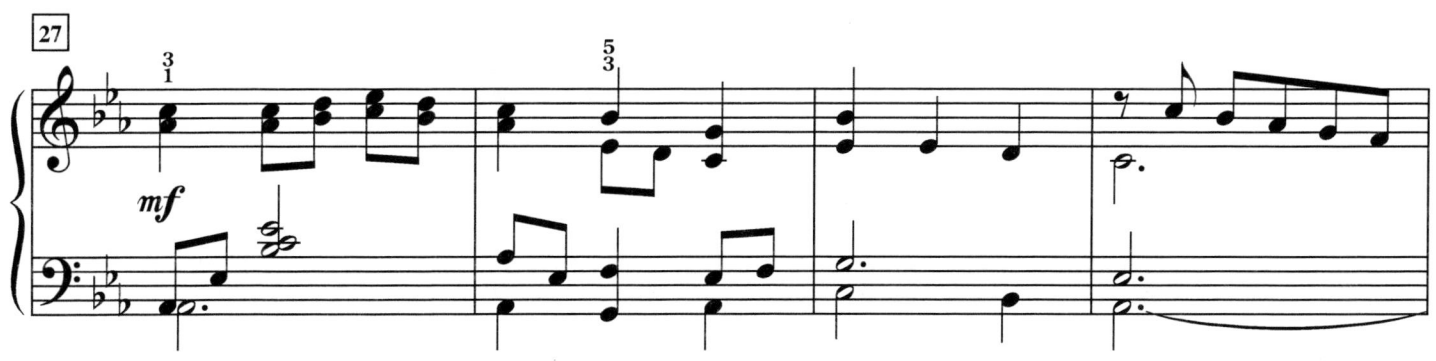

Sun of My Soul

Words by John Keble

Sun of my soul, Thou Savior dear,
It is not night if Thou be near;
O may no earthborn cloud arise
To hide Thee from Thy servant's eyes.

from *Katholisches Gesangbuch*
Arr. Tom Fettke

36

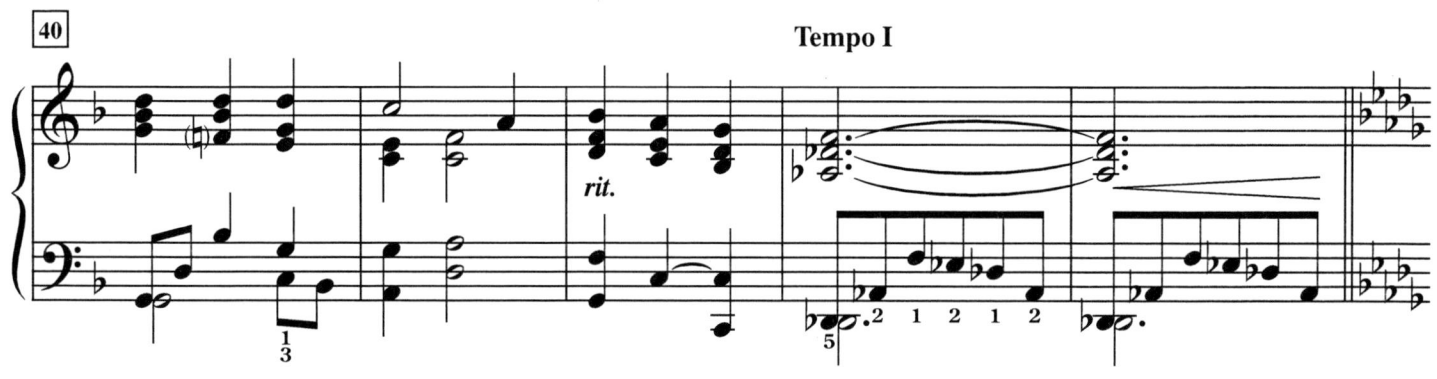

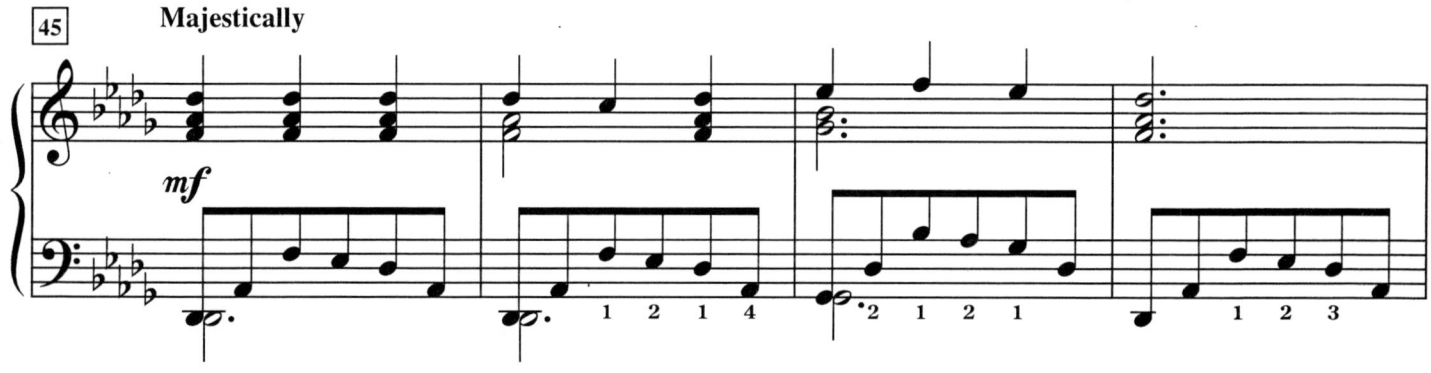